MICHIGAN STATE SPARTANS

BY

MARGARET WEBER

INSIDE COLLEGE FOOTBALL

MEDIA ENHANCED BOOKS AV² BY WEIGL ADDED VALUE • AUDIO VISUAL

www.av2books.com

Published by AV^{2} by Weigl
350 5th Avenue, 59th Floor
New York, NY 10118
Website: www.av2books.com

Library of Congress Control Number: 2018968203

ISBN 978-1-7911-0087-2 (hardcover)
ISBN 978-1-7911-0088-9 (multi-user eBook)
ISBN 978-1-7911-0089-6 (single-user eBook)

Printed in Guangzhou, China
1 2 3 4 5 6 7 8 9 0 23 22 21 20 19

042019
102318

Project Coordinator: Jared Siemens Designer: Terry Paulhus

Every reasonable effort has been made to trace ownership and to obtain permission to reprint copyright material. The publishers would be pleased to have any errors or omissions brought to their attention so that they may be corrected in subsequent printings.

The publisher acknowledges Alamy, Getty Images, Newscom, Flickr CC, and Wikimedia Commons as its primary image suppliers for this title.

INSIDE COLLEGE FOOTBALL

Michigan State Spartans

CONTENTS

Introduction

College football began at Michigan State in 1885. The first team played as part of the Michigan Intercollegiate Athletic Association after it became a varsity sport in 1896. This team would give rise to the Michigan State Spartans, who left the league in 1907.

Today, the Spartans are part of the Big Ten Conference. They have won 11 conference **championships** since 1903. The team is known for its **rivalries** against schools such as Pennsylvania State University and the University of Notre Dame. Each time the Spartans play the University of Notre Dame, the two teams compete for the Megaphone Trophy. One side of the trophy is blue for Notre Dame and one side is green for Michigan State. This shows the history of wins and losses for both teams. These championships and **traditions** show the Spartans to be a strong team that is always striving to be greater.

Michigan State backup quarterback Rocky Lombardi made his first appearance for the team as a punter during a 2018 game against Arizona State University.

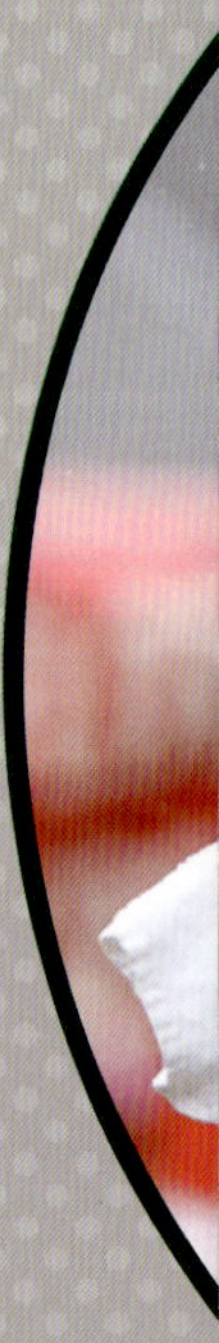

Offensive lineman Matt Allen is the youngest of three brothers to play the same position on Michigan State's football team. Allen logged 48 snaps in his first year on the field for the Spartans.

MICHIGAN STATE

Stadium	Spartan Stadium
Division	Big Ten East
Head Coach	Mark Dantonio
Location	East Lansing, Michigan
National Championships	1
Nicknames	Spartans

28
Bowl Appearances

94
Seasons Played by 2018

31
Consensus All-American Players

36
First-Round NFL Draft Picks

History

The Spartans' longest **winning streak** at home was 19 games, between 1950 and 1953.

Halfback Clinton Jones rushed for 784 yards and made 159 carries in 1966, his final year with the Spartans. Jones went on to play seven seasons in the National Football League (NFL).

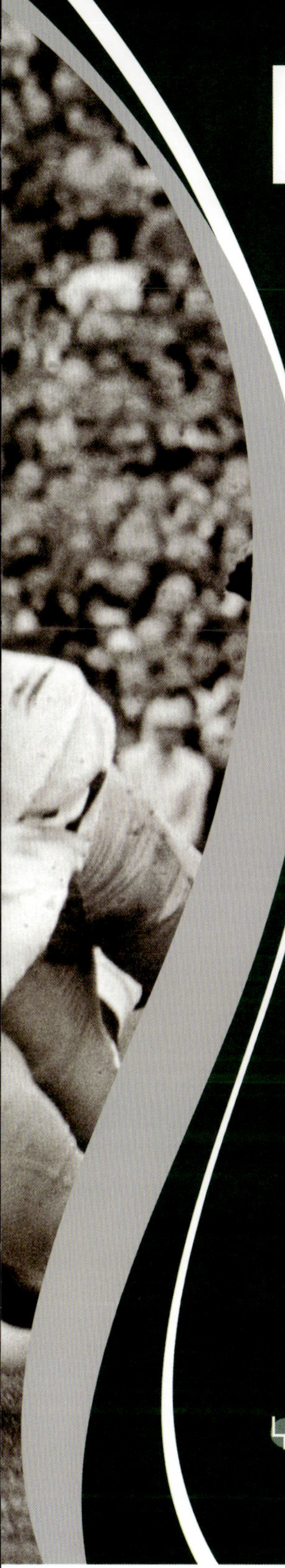

Michigan State was among the first colleges to field a football team. The school was originally known as Michigan Agricultural College. The history of the Spartans is also part of the history of football itself. Chester Brewer was an early coach who impacted how football is played. He was seen as a defensive **genius** and held a record of 58 wins during his time.

In 1925, the school officially changed its name to Michigan State University (MSU). Until then, the team had been known as the Aggies. A *Lansing State Journal* reporter named George S. Alderton held a contest to rename the university's sports teams. The Spartans name won, and has been a part of the university ever since.

The Spartans joined the Big Ten in 1953. Throughout the 1950s and 1960s, the Spartans were a football force to be reckoned with. In 1966, the Spartans were ranked second in the country. They faced off against Notre Dame, the number-one ranked team at the time. By the second quarter, the Spartans led 10–0. However, Notre Dame battled back and the game ended in a 10–10 tie. Today, fans still consider it the "Game of the Century." Since then, the Spartans have continued to be an important team in college football.

The 1966 tie against top-ranked Notre Dame gave the Spartans first place in the Big Ten.

The Stadium

Michigan State University is home to one of the top turfgrass management programs in the country. Students in the program care for the 72,000 square feet (6,689 sq. m) of natural grass on the field at Spartan Stadium.

Since 1923, Spartan Stadium has served as home for the players and fans of the Michigan State Spartans. It was built to replace Old College Field. The original name for the stadium was Macklin Stadium. The name was changed in 1957, at the same time that seating was expanded. The stadium is both historic and modern, having been **renovated** in 2005 and 2014. The playing field is grass. The grass was replaced in 2011 after the field was ruined when the stadium hosted a concert by the rock band U2.

Watching a game at Spartan Field is an exciting experience. Since 1957, there have been 170 games where crowds have reached the stadium's capacity. The record attendance was set in 1990 when 80,401 fans watched a game against Notre Dame. Today, fans enjoy high-definition screens and an LED ribbon board that is 450 feet (137 meters) long.

The Spartans are strongest when they play at home. Michigan State has seen 30 seasons with only one home game loss at Spartan Stadium. This tradition of winning at home is why more than 63,000 season tickets were sold in 2012.

The 5,300-square-foot (492-sq.-m) end zone scoreboard at Spartan Stadium is the largest screen in the state of Michigan. It is almost 10 times bigger than the Spartans' original scoreboard.

Where They Play

Welcome to Spartan Stadium. Die-hard fans turn out rain or shine to cheer on their team. For almost a century, crowds of more than 70,000 have filled the stadium for home football games. A winning team, a top marching band, and many fan traditions make Spartan Stadium one of college football's best.

BIG TEN WEST

1. **Northwestern University**
   Evanston, Illinois
2. **Purdue University**
   West Lafayette, Indiana
3. **University of Illinois**
   Urbana-Champaign, Illinois
4. **University of Iowa**
   Iowa City, Iowa
5. **University of Minnesota**
   Minneapolis, Minnesota
6. **University of Nebraska**
   Lincoln, Nebraska
7. **University of Wisconsin**
   Madison, Wisconsin

Arena
Spartan Stadium

Location
East Lansing, Michigan

Broke Ground
1923

Completed
1923

Surface
Real Grass

Features
- There are 24 luxury boxes
- Fan capacity is just more than 75,000
- The LED ribbon board in the north end zone is 10 feet (3 m) high

BIG TEN EAST

1. **Indiana University**
   Bloomington, Indiana
2. ★ **Michigan State University**
   East Lansing, Michigan
3. **Ohio State University**
   Columbus, Ohio
4. **Pennsylvania State University**
   State College, Pennsylvania
5. **Rutgers University–New Brunswick**
   New Brunswick–Piscataway, New Jersey
6. **University of Maryland**
   College Park, Maryland
7. **University of Michigan**
   Ann Arbor, Michigan

NORTH DAKOTA
MINNESOTA
SOUTH DAKOTA
WISCONSIN
MICHIGAN
NEBRASKA
IOWA
ILLINOIS
INDIANA
OHIO
KANSAS
MISSOURI
KENTUCKY
WEST VIRGINIA
VIRGINIA
PENNSYLVANIA
NEW YORK
RHODE ISLAND
CONNECTICUT
NEW JERSEY
DELAWARE
MARYLAND
WASHINGTON, D.C.
NORTH CAROLINA
TENNESSEE
SOUTH CAROLINA
OKLAHOMA
ARKANSAS
MISSISSIPPI
ALABAMA
GEORGIA
TEXAS
LOUISIANA
FLORIDA
Atlantic Ocean
Gulf of Mexico
SCALE
0 miles
500 miles
0 kilometers
500 km
LEGEND
Home Stadium
Big Ten West
Big Ten East
United States
Other Countries
Water

The Uniforms

Michigan State head coach **Mark Dantonio** has changed the team's jersey and helmet **colors** four times since his arrival in 2007.

The Spartans debuted an all-white look, including a white helmet, in a game against Western Michigan on September 9, 2017.

Although the Spartans wore black and gold uniforms for a few seasons in the 1930s, Michigan State's official colors are green and white. The Spartans typically play home games in green jerseys with white accents. Player numbers are on the front and back, and on both sleeves of the jerseys. Their home uniform pants are either white with green accents, or green with white accents. The Spartans' all-white away uniform debuted in 1939, and it has been the official away uniform ever since.

HOME

AWAY

Michigan State's helmets are usually green, although players sometimes take the field in an alternate white or bronze helmet. These helmets are part of the team's alternate uniforms, which are worn for special games. In 2011, the Spartans debuted a Nike "Pro Combat" uniform for their game against the Michigan Wolverines. The all-green uniform has black and bronze accents and a bronze helmet. Coach Mark Dantonio is known for making changes to the team's uniform combinations, and both players and fans enjoy the team's ever-changing look.

The Spartans have been wearing their trademark green helmets for more than 50 years. Minor changes over time have included the helmets' finish and the style of the Spartan logo on the side.

Student Athletes

Instead of a single team **captain**, the Spartans rotate through a group of 12, known as the leadership group.

Players such as tight end Matt Dotson compete with teammates for starting positions on the field. Dotson played in 10 games as a freshman, and all 13 games as a sophomore.

Being a college student athlete is hard work. Student athletes have to perform well on the football field and in the classroom. They are required to meet a minimum grade point average and attend all of their classes. Student athletes have very busy schedules between classes, practices, and games, both at home and away from campus. The Student-Athlete Support Services office works to provide academic services and support to student athletes. In 2002, the office set a record when 22 Spartans were chosen as Academic All-Big Ten selections.

Many student athletes are given athletic scholarships. An athletic scholarship is an agreement between the athlete and the college or university. Athletes who do not receive an athletic scholarship can be "walk-on" members of the team. This means they are on the team, but without athletic financial aid. Michigan State typically awards the maximum number of football scholarships allowed, which is 85.

Jordan Reid played in all 13 games for the Spartans as a true freshman in 2017. Reid is one of Michigan State's 85 football scholarship recipients.

Bowl Games

Percy Snow made **17 tackles** in the 1988 **Rose Bowl**, the record number of bowl-game tackles in Spartan history.

Michigan came back from a 20-point deficit to defeat Baylor University 42–41 in the 2015 Cotton Bowl.

After the college football season ends, a rare sports tradition begins. The National Collegiate Athletic Association (NCAA) does not sponsor a **postseason** for the sport of football. Instead, a variety of games called bowl games are played. There are currently 40 bowl games played between college football teams. These games give teams the chance to play rivals or new teams. It is also a chance to compete for respect and wins even after they have finished with the regular season.

The Spartans' first bowl appearance was in the Orange Bowl in 1938. Since then, they have played in a variety of postseason games. They are one of only four teams to ever play in the short-lived Cherry Bowl. In the Silicon Valley Bowl, the Spartans set their personal record for bowl passes and rushes. Coach Mark Dantonio has taken the Michigan State Spartans to more bowl games than any other coach in MSU history. Under his leadership, the Spartans have played in a total of 11 bowl games.

The Spartans' regular-season finish of 9–3 landed them a spot in the 2017 Holiday Bowl, where they defeated Washington State Cougars 42–17.

The Coaches

Coach Dantonio led the Spartans to their first **13-win season** in team history in 2013.

MSU head coach Mark Dantonio's contract automatically renews every six years, which means he is a "Spartan for life" unless he decides to take a coaching job somewhere else.

The very first coach of the Michigan State Spartans varsity team, Henry Keep, was also one of the team's players. Since then, the coaches have all been professionals who took on the role of leading and guiding the team to victory. The greatest coaches in Spartan history led their teams to winning seasons and exciting postseasons, and left **legacies** that the team and fans still celebrate today.

CLARENCE "BIGGIE" MUNN Clarence "Biggie" Munn coached the Spartans from 1947 to 1953. In 1951 and 1952, his hard work paid off for the team. Michigan State went undefeated in two back-to-back seasons. It was a sign that Munn had brought the team to the national stage. This success helped propel the formerly independent Spartans into the Big Ten Conference.

DUFFY DAUGHERTY Duffy Daugherty served as head coach from 1954 to 1972. He was one of the first coaches to bring African American players to Michigan State University. He is remembered for winning the Rose Bowl in only his second year leading the team. By bringing together talented players, Daugherty was able to become the winningest coach in Spartan history. When he retired from coaching in 1972, he had 109 wins.

MARK DANTONIO Spartans fans have enjoyed watching their team win since Mark Dantonio took over as head coach in 2007. Between 2007 and 2018, the Spartans have posted winning records in 10 seasons out of 12. Dantonio has had success winning both the Rose Bowl and the Cotton Bowl. He also won two Big Ten titles. With 100 wins to his name, he has his eye on breaking the winningest coach record.

The Mascot

Sparty was voted America's "Buffest Mascot" by *Muscle & Fitness* magazine, and has been named the national champion of mascots three times by the Universal Cheer Association.

The Michigan State mascot, Sparty, is a Spartan solider. Michigan State takes its nickname from the Spartans, warriors from ancient Greece. Sparty is dressed in armor and also wears green and white. The very first mascot was made from papier-mâché and was created by members of the Theta Xi **fraternity**. This mascot was used from 1955 to 1956, when it was replaced by a similar mascot made from fiberglass.

In 1982, Sparty became the costumed mascot that is now recognized on the field. In the late 1980s, the MSU Alumni Association held a contest to redesign the mascot. After conducting some research, the university introduced the new Sparty in 1989. The university describes Sparty as being an "approachable, fierce yet kind, man for all seasons."

Sparty gets his name from two Spartan warrior statues on the campus of Michigan State University. One is made of terra cotta clay, and the other is an exact replica made of bronze.

Legends of the Past

For many players, their time with the Spartans is the start of a promising football career. These are some of the best-known football players to play for Michigan State.

Le'Veon Bell

From his first year at Michigan State, fans knew that Le'Veon Bell would be an important player for the Spartans. As a freshman, he played in 13 games. He was also awarded All-Big Ten Freshman honors. In his sophomore year, he had a total of 13 touchdowns. Bell ran for 253 yards in 2012. This earned him the honor of being voted onto the first-team All-Big Ten. In 2013, he joined the NFL **draft**. He was selected in the second round by the Pittsburgh Steelers, where he continues to play today.

Position: Running Back
Seasons: 2010–2012 (Michigan State Spartans), 2013–Present (Pittsburgh Steelers)
Born: February 18, 1992, Reynoldsburg, Ohio

Darqueze Dennard

In his freshman year as a Spartan, Darqueze Dennard played in six games. He experienced a short **setback** when an injury kept him out of five games. Eager to prove himself, Dennard came back in his sophomore year to play in 11 games. In his junior year, he started in all 13 games. This determination won him admiration across college football. He was awarded the **Jim Thorpe Award** in his senior year. He was drafted by the Cincinnati Bengals in 2014 and was the only Spartan to join an NFL team that year. Dennard remains a part of the Bengals' defense.

Position: Cornerback
Seasons: 2010–2013 (Michigan State Spartans), 2014–Present (Cincinnati Bengals)
Born: October 10, 1991, Dry Branch, Georgia

Trae Waynes

When Trae Waynes began his career at Michigan State, he did not see a lot of time on the field. This changed by his sophomore year, when he started in 14 games and was an All-Big Ten pick. He also led his team to a Rose Bowl victory. In 2014, he started in every game. Waynes was a finalist for the Jim Thorpe Award in his senior year. In 2015, Waynes entered the NFL draft. At that time, he was seen as one of the best cornerbacks in the country and was chosen by the Minnesota Vikings.

Position: Cornerback
Seasons: 2011–2014 (Michigan State Spartans), 2015–Present (Minnesota Vikings)
Born: July 25, 1992, Kenosha, Wisconsin

Jack Conklin

Jack Conklin started in 38 out of 39 games he played as a Michigan Spartan. This may have come as a surprise considering that Conklin was never recruited by a Michigan State coach. Instead, he joined the team as a walk-on player. His commitment to football paid off for the Spartans. In 2015, Conklin was named first-team **All-American**. He decided to forgo his senior year in order to join the NFL draft. Conklin was chosen eighth overall by the Tennessee Titans.

Position: Offensive Tackle
Seasons: 2013–2015 (Michigan State Spartans), 2016–Present (Tennessee Titans)
Born: August 17, 1994, Plainwell, Michigan

All-Time Records

28
Longest Win Streak
Michigan State's longest consecutive winning streak was 28 games, which began in 1950 and ended in 1953.

38
Biggest Comeback Win
The Spartans had their biggest comeback ever against Northwestern University in 2006 when they came from behind to win 41–38.

25
Largest Bowl Victory
Michigan State saw a bowl victory margin of 25, its largest ever, when the Spartans defeated Washington State in the 2017 Holiday Bowl with a score of 42–17.

9,194

Most Rushing Yards

Connor Cook holds the record for most yards run as a Michigan Spartan, with 9,194.

74

Most Career Touchdowns

Connor Cook scored 74 touchdowns between 2012 and 2015 while playing for the Spartans.

Throughout the team's history, the Michigan State Spartans have had many memorable events that have become defining moments for the team and its fans.

1965
In 1965, the Michigan State Spartans finish 10–0 and are ranked number one in NCAA football at the end of the regular season.

In 1903, Chester Brewer becomes coach and brings in a new era of strong defense.

1900 1920 1940 1960

1951
The 1951 Spartan team, coached by Clarence Munn, goes undefeated through the regular season.

1955–1963
Between 1955 and 1963, the Spartans beat rival Notre Dame eight times in a row.

1953
The Michigan State Spartans join the Big Ten in 1953.

The Future

The Michigan Spartans are a competitive team that is looking to claim more National Championships and winning seasons. Dantonio is concentrating on building a strong defense in order to make his team one of the best in the country. As fans continue to flock to East Lansing to attend games and cheer on the team, they can expect to see a bright future.

1966

The Spartans face off against Notre Dame in the Game of the Century in 1966 and tie 10–10.

2008-2017

From 2008 to 2017, MSU wins a record eight games over their rivals, the Michigan Wolverines.

1980

2000

2020

1998

The Michigan State Spartans come back from low years with a 1998 win over first-ranked Ohio State University.

In 2007, Mark Dantonio takes the field as head coach.

Write a Biography

Life Story

A person's life story can be the subject of a book. This kind of book is called a biography. Biographies often describe the lives of people who have achieved great success. These people may be alive today, or they may have lived many years ago. Reading a biography can help you learn more about a great person.

Get the Facts

Use this book, and research in the library and on the internet, to find out more about your favorite player. Learn as much about him as you can. What position does he play? What are his statistics in important categories? Has he set any records? Also, be sure to write down key events in the person's life. What was his childhood like? What has he accomplished off the field? Is there anything else that makes this person special or unusual?

Use the Concept Web

A concept web is a useful research tool. Read the questions in the concept web on the following page. Answer the questions in your notebook. Your answers will help you write a biography.

Concept Web

Write a Biography

Adulthood
- Where does this individual currently reside?
- Does he have a family?

Your Opinion
- What did you learn from the books you read in your research?
- Would you suggest these books to others?
- Was anything missing from these books?

Childhood
- Where and when was this person born?
- Describe his parents, siblings, and friends.
- Did he grow up in unusual circumstances?

Accomplishments off the Field
- What is this person's life's work?
- Has he received awards or recognition for accomplishments?
- How have this person's accomplishments served others?

Help and Obstacles
- Did this individual have a positive attitude?
- Did he receive help from others?
- Did this person have a mentor?
- Did this person face any hardships?
- If so, how were the hardships overcome?

Accomplishments on the Field
- What records does this person hold?
- What key games and plays have defined his career?
- What are his stats in categories important to his position?

Work and Preparation
- What was this person's education?
- What was his work experience?
- How does this person work?
- What is the process he uses?

Trivia Time

Take this quiz to test your knowledge of the Michigan State Spartans. The answers are printed upside down under each question.

1 When did college football begin for Michigan State?

A. 1885

2 Which conference does the team play in?

A. The Big Ten Conference

3 Which city is Spartan Stadium in?

A. East Lansing

4 How many bowl appearances have the Spartans made?

A. 28

5 What was the Spartans' longest winning streak at home?

A. 28 games between 1950 and 1953

6 Which rival team do the Spartans play for the Megaphone Trophy?

A. The University of Notre Dame

7 How many National Championships have the Spartans won?

A. One

8 When did Spartan Stadium open?

A. 1923

9 What are the Spartans' colors?

A. Green and white

10 When did the Spartans first play in a bowl game?

A. In 1938 in the Orange Bowl

Key Words

All-American: a player, usually in high school or college, judged to be the best in each position of a sport

championships: contests that determine top performers for a sport or activity

draft: an annual event where the NFL chooses college football players to be new team members

fraternity: an exclusive society made up of male students at a university

genius: a person who is very smart or creative

Jim Thorpe Award: an award given to the top defensive back in college football

legacies: something handed down by a previous generation

postseason: a sporting event that takes place after the end of the regular season

renovated: improved or expanded an older building

rivalries: competitions between different groups or individuals toward the same objective or goal

setback: when progress has been reversed

traditions: customs or beliefs that are passed from one generation to another

Index

Log on to www.av2books.com

AV² by Weigl brings you media enhanced books that support active learning. Go to www.av2books.com, and enter the special code found on page 2 of this book. You will gain access to enriched and enhanced content that supplements and complements this book. Content includes video, audio, weblinks, quizzes, a slideshow, and activities.

AV² Online Navigation

Audio
Listen to sections of the book read aloud.

Book Pages
AV² pages directly correspond to pages in the book.

Video
Watch informative video clips.

Embedded Weblinks
Gain additional information for research.

Key Words
Study vocabulary, and complete a matching word activity.

Try This!
Complete activities and hands-on experiments.

Quizzes
Test your knowledge.

Slideshow
View images and captions, and prepare a presentation.

AV² was built to bridge the gap between print and digital. We encourage you to tell us what you like and what you want to see in the future.

Sign up to be an AV² Ambassador at www.av2books.com/ambassador.

Due to the dynamic nature of the internet, some of the URLs and activities provided as part of AV² by Weigl may have changed or ceased to exist. AV² by Weigl accepts no responsibility for any such changes. All media enhanced books are regularly monitored to update addresses and sites in a timely manner. Contact AV² by Weigl at 1-866-649-3445 or av2books@weigl.com with any questions, comments, or feedback.